AUTHOR'S NOTE

I heard BTS' music for the first time in 2017. They had just relea-sed their fifth EP, *Love Yourself* 承 *'Her'* on September 18th of that year. Soon afterwards, I mentioned BTS to Jaesung Lee, the host of the radio program I had been on every Sunday morning for the past four years. His response was, "You know BTS?" He was rather surprised by the fact that an old-fashioned, middle-aged music critic like myself would have ever noticed and appreciated a youthful sensation like BTS. My impre-ssion of the boy group however, was quite strong. I personally thought they were extremely talented, and I wanted to learn more about the seven boys and their music.

When *Love Yourself* 承 *'Her'* was released, it became a huge su-ccess. With "DNA" as the lead single, the album had sold over 1.6 million physical copies as of March 2018 and had also broken the record for the highest number of album pre-orders sold. BTS' album left an impactful mark in the American music industry by debuting at number seven on the Billboard 200 Albums Chart. It remained at the top of the chart for six whole weeks, and although it momentarily fell, it quickly rose back up the following month. At the same time, "DNA" was at number 67 on the Billboard Hot 100 Chart. This made BTS the first South Korean artist to be on both the Billboard Hot 100 Chart and the Billboard 200 Albums Chart simultaneously for four consecutive weeks. BTS' achievement was an amazing, as well as thrilling milestone for the South Korean music industry.

This book is fully and strictly focused on reviewing BTS' albums. In an interview with Rolling Stone magazine in 1969, Jim Morrison of the Doors stated, "No one can remember an entire novel. No one can des-cribe a film, a piece of sculpture, a painting. But so long as there are hu-man beings, songs and poetry can continue" (Hopkins, 1969). Why do I mention poetry and songs? Why do I insist on reviewing the albums of the 'biggest boy band in the world'? It is because I believe that BTS is the preeminent pop icon of the 21st Century. My old friend, Pilwon Lee, popular singer and songwriter of the 1970s, once said, "The only thing that will remain for an artist is their albums." I agree with this statement. Songs and albums tell stories of the artist, and those stories will remain forever as long as there are people to remember them. I hope BTS will be evermore celebrated and cherished by future generations as their musical accomplishments reach all around the world.

PREFACE

BTS' music represents the outcries of the Millennials and the Generation Zers. Due to the social and financial constraints in present-day South Korean society, much of today's youth has given up on the idea of the typical traditional life concept of getting into a relationship, getting married, and ultimately having children. BTS' Bangtan music or "bulletproof music" (Bangtan in Korean meaning bulletproof) not only carries the group's own blood, sweat, and tears, but it also reflects the outcries and screams of the younger generation of our society. Their albums tell the stories of the group's seven members; stories that much of today's youth can directly relate to. I would like to lay out their musical spirits in this book so that the readers may not only feel BTS' aspirations and dreams, but also share their yearnings for freedom, peace, and a world made brighter with their music and performances.

On December 13th, 2017, "DNA" ranked number 49 on the Billboard Hot 100 Chart—this made it the highest-charting entry by a K-Pop artist or group on the Billboard Hot 100 Chart. The critics claimed that this was no coincidence that BTS had successfully broken through the U.S. music industry since their debut in 2013. Many believed BTS was a rare case of K-Pop influencing the Western music scene. It was interesting that a South Korean boy band who grew up listening and dancing to American Pop music, would go on to influence the Western music industry today, which shows how the boys have come a long way.

BTS ended the year 2017 by performing at the annual New Year's Eve broadcast of the television special "*Dick Clark's New Year's Rockin' Eve*" on ABC. This was the second time a Korean artist was part of the show ever since Psy's performance with "Gangnam Style" in 2012. BTS' performance was explosive, and their fan base, ARMY, anticipated a bigger and more impactful new year for the boys: Jin, Suga, J-Hope, RM, Jimin, V, and Jungkook.

German philosopher Georg Wilhelm Friedrich Hegel once said, "Nothing great in the world has ever been accomplished without passion." About a year and a half ago, I was impressed by BTS' powerful music and perfectly synchronized dance performances. Now that I have heard all of their songs, seen their performances, and reviewed their albums, I am even more excited and delighted by their passion and success. I would like to dedicate this book to BTS, and I hope that their music will become immortal like a timeless piece of art.

BTS

WELCOME,
FIRST TIME WITH BTS?

PART

1

●

I want to play and eat
I want to tear the school uniform

Uncertainty in my bank account
My misery is over the limit

Grown-ups tell me this
Put up with it only for now
Tolerate it just a little longer
Deal with it later

Everybody say NO!

Later doesn't work any more
Don't be locked up in others' dreams any more

O! RUL8, 2? (Oh, are you late, too?)
Track 2 "N.O"
Released in September 2013

Chapter 1

BTS earns their first No.1 album on the Billboard 200 Chart
with Love Yourself: Her

On May 20th, 2018, BTS performed onstage at the 2018 Billboard
Music Awards after winning the Top Social Artist award for the second
year running. They beat out superstars such as Justin Bieber, Demi Lo-
vato, Ariana Grande, and Shawn Mendes to be recognized as the artist
with the most fan engagement on social platforms.

Upon accepting the award, RM addressed the roaring crowd and
said, "Thank you so much Billboard Music Awards for this precious award
for two years in a row. This time we had a chance to think about what
'social' really means for us. Some of our fans told us that our music really
changed their lives, and now we realize that our words truly carry weight
thanks to you guys. ARMYs out there, you guys, your words keep us going and keep us striving!" Jimin spoke next in Korean, "It's ARMYs who
won this award. Thank you, and we love you." After the award show,
instead of attending the Star-studded afterparty, BTS met with their fans
via a live broadcast (V-Live) and had a party of their own. According to
J-Hope, "As usual, we wanted to see our fans after the big accomplishment, so we had an afterparty with our ARMYs worldwide." On BTS'
win at the Billboard Music Awards, South Korean President Jae-In Moon con-
gratulated them through a special message on social media sites. He said,
"BTS' music is sincere…They have a magical ability to turn sadness into
hope and differences into similarity. Congratulations to the seven boys
who love music and their ARMYs who have been the wings for the boys."

Rolling Stone magazine reported on the unique quality of the group.
"[BTS has been] speaking their minds since their debut, openly discussing
LGBTQ rights, mental health issues, and the pressure to succeed–all ta-
boo subjects in South Korea… By straddling the line between maintaining a respectable image and writing critical lyrics, BTS have offered a
refreshing change from what some critics and fans dislike about the K-Pop
machine-like music industry" (Kim, 2018). The featured article went on to

mention how openly the members of BTS show support and generosity towards both social issues, as well as the most controversial political scandals in South Korea such as the Sewol Ferry tragedy. While many politicians and social leaders were busy trying to distance themselves from the Sewol Ferry tragedy, BTS supported the victims' families by donating $100,000. Their involvement in politically charged incidents continues with the time when BTS raised $1 million with ARMYs in less than two days for UNICEF (United Nations Children's Fund) while partnering with the organization for an anti-violence campaign. Sometime afterwards, Suga donated $19,000 worth of beef to feed orphans on his 25th birthday on behalf of ARMY—this triggered chain reactions from fans around the globe who made their own charitable donations.

During an interview on *CNN Today* in 2018, K-Pop columnist for Billboard, Jeff Benjamin, expressed his view on the significance of BTS leading the Billboard 200 Chart by saying, "This is a huge win for BTS, but this is also a huge win for global music at large. America is the biggest music industry in the world, and this is a huge step showing that Americans are opening their eyes, opening their minds, opening their ears to great music that doesn't necessarily need to be in English… BTS, their music itself, it has messages, it has a concept, it has symbols that go beyond language and that transcend culture… BTS says something larger than just K-Pop music".

Now BTS may be the hottest boy group with mega hits and loyal fans all over the world, but they seem to be able to remain calm and humble. They still share the same house, except it is bigger and more luxurious than before, and their bond seems to be stronger than ever. They also sometimes wonder where they would have been if BTS had never formed. The boys appeared on the SBS 8 O'clock News in South Korea on June 3rd, 2018. During the studio interview they were asked, "What would you be doing now if you didn't become a member of BTS?"

Jimin: "When I was in 9th grade, I had a tough time deciding between two options. I either wanted to become a policeman or a stage performer. I chose to be a performer, but if I hadn't, I might have wanted to become a policeman."

V: "I wanted to become someone like my father more than anything else. When I started dreaming to become a singer, I picked up an instrument, the saxophone, and I took lessons for three years. However, I have stopped playing for eight years now, but I could have become a saxophonist."

J-Hope: "I used to love playing tennis in elementary school. I could have been a tennis player if I hadn't pursued music."

Suga: "Producer... that's how I joined the company in the first place, as a producer. So, probably I would be a producer... or, maybe a newscaster... (pointing at the host) I could be sitting in your seat."

When Suga was a trainee, he got involved in a terrible accident which almost ended his career as a performer before it had even begun. To pay for his school tuition, Suga worked part time as a delivery boy riding a small motorcycle. When the accident happened, he said he remembers seeing the tires of a car right in front of his face, and then next thing he knew, he could not move his shoulder. He later found out that his shoulder had been crushed, and the severity of the injury resulted in him deciding to stop training as a trainee. BTS' management agency, Big Hit Entertainment, eventually found out about this accident and told him that they would wait for him until he got better and even paid for Suga's school tuition—something that Suga is still very thankful for today.

V was named the world's most handsome man in 2017 by TC Candler's Annual Independent Critics List of the 100 Most Beautiful Faces and 100 Most Handsome Faces of the Year. He beat out American actors like Jason Momoa and Armie Hammer. Jungkook and Jimin were also included in the list at 13th and 64th, respectively.

At some point before their debut, J-Hope had dropped out of BTS. He had hit a slump and was feeling depressed as a trainee. Big Hit Entertainment, however, didn't look for his replacement and patiently waited for J-Hope and convinced him to come back.

The youngest member, Jungkook, who showed off his lean and sleek abs on stage during the 2018 Billboard Music Awards, almost didn't become a member of BTS. During a V-Live, Jimin revealed a story of when Jungkook returned from his trip to America, he told Jimin he might stop being a trainee and go under his dance teacher as his apprentice instead because he felt really passionate about dancing. After being persuaded by Jimin, he gave up the short-lived dream and held on to become the center position of the group.

Jin was streetcast (spotted and approached by a talent agent in the streets) while he was on his way to his school's campus during his freshman year at Konkuk University where he was majoring in Theatre and Film. He is a self-proclaimed 'world class good-looking man' and wanted to be an actor but ended up signing with Big Hit Entertainment as a member of BTS. During the 2017 BTS "DNA" Comeback Show, Jin introduced his pets, two small sugar gliders named Uhmook and Odeng (both meaning fishcake in Korean) to his fans. He was initially worried to show his pets to the younger ARMYs in case they tried to follow suit and adopt sugar gliders without proper knowledge and preparation. He stated that one should raise pets when they are ready to take on the full responsibility of taking care of the animals.

When Wolfgang Amadeus Mozart had no firewood for the stove, he was known to hold his wife's hand, dance to warm himself up, and continue writing music in the cold. It was the most beautiful musical epistle sent under the most unfortunate conditions. BTS also went through difficult times as trainees. They danced and sang as if they were walking into a future as vague as a mirage, but somehow, like magic, people around the world started paying attention to them. "I Need U", the lead single for their third EP album *The Most Beautiful Moment in Life Part 1*, made their presence known. Then came the tracks "Dope" and "Fire", both of which are included in album *The Most Beautiful Moment in Life: Young Forever* the third compilation album released on May 2nd, 2016. With these songs, BTS expressed their strong feelings for fighting against all prejudice and suppression whilst moving forward for their dreams.

"Blood Sweat & Tears", a track from the second studio album *Wings*, was inspired by the novel *Demian*, by the German writer, Hermann Hesse. The novel portrays a troubled young man's quest for self-awareness. If that story reflected the growing pains which BTS themselves encountered, their fans understood. When "DNA" was released, many people in different parts of the world were chanting, "All these are not coincidence" and "We are together forever" in Korean alongside BTS. Now with their new single, "Fake Love", the boys call us into a special space where we can taste sadness, experience precious beauty, and become slowly addicted to their music. BTS brings tears to their listeners' eyes and makes people sing along and feel as if they're walking on clouds. It is no surprise to hear about how quickly their concert tickets sell out. The BTS World Tour, a total of 33 concerts, which will be held between August 25th and October 20th, 2018 in South Korea, the United States, Canada, the United Kingdom, the Netherlands, Germany, France, and five other countries, sold

out within just a few minutes of the pre-sale box office opening. In Berlin,
scalpers ticket were being sold for over $4,000. Where there are fans,
there are also haters. Of course, BTS has haters too. The boys, however,
seem to maintain their cool even towards those who express disapproval
and hostility.

●

You're a drain and I'm amused
Kids with their talent on strike
Protest awful lot behind my back
Man, what you afraid of
I'm confident on top of the beat

From Daegu to Apgujeong, I've spread out my beat
Here and there, all around the world, my music is alive
I'm a baby shaman who dances on the open blade,
that's me (that's me)

While you people are playing around
We are going around the world

Dark & Wild
Track 7 "Cypher Pt. 3: Killer"
Released in August 2014

Chapter 2

BTS
2 COOL 4 SKOOL

On June 12th, 2013, BTS released their debut single album *2 Cool 4 Skool*. The album included seven songs plus two hidden tracks only available on the physical copy of the albums.

1. Intro: 2 Cool 4 Skool (featuring DJ Friz) (1:03)
2. We Are Bulletproof, Pt. 2 (3:43)
3. Skit: Circle Room Talk (2:11)
4. No More Dream (3:42)
5. Interlude (0:52)
6. I Like It (3:51)
7. Outro: Circle Room Cypher (5:21)

Bonus Tracks:
8. Skit: On the Start Line
9. Gil (Road/Path)

Intro: "2 Cool 4 Skool (featuring DJ Friz)"

The sound of the drums makes my heart pound. It is an important element that moves people emotionally, especially those who are oppressed. The people of South Korea have often stormed the streets and cried out, "Prohibit the command that prohibits." It has happened time after time throughout the country's history.

The March 1st Independence Movement on March 1st, 1919; the April Revolution of April 19th, 1960; the Gwangju Democratic Uprising on May 18th, 1980; the June Democracy Movement in 1987; the Candlelight Revolution during the winter of 2016 through the spring of 2017. The drumbeats helped the peaceful march of the people and pushed them to advance towards victory.

In the book, *The Seven Years of General Yi Soon Shin*, written by Korean novelist Chan-Joo Jeong, Jeong describes the beating of the drums that accompanied General Yi's last moments alive. When the Japanese bullet penetrated General Yi's heart, he told his eldest son to continue beating the drums so that the soldiers would not know of his death and to proceed with the battle. "Don't let them know I'm dead." I interpret those last words from General Yi as a promise that he would never die and that he would always protect Korea from foreign invaders whatever the situation is.

When BTS sing, it is like a declaration that they will fight against the discrimination, injustice, and unfairness caused by social prejudice and misconceptions; it is a promise that they will reach out to those who are less fortunate, neglected, and isolated. For that, the name Bangtan Boys perfectly suits their objectives.

We Are Bulletproof, Pt. 2

By the year 2013, there were plenty of boy groups and idol stars in South Korea, but no one had heard such intense and radical sounds like BTS until the second track "We Are Bulletproof Pt.2" from the album *2 Cool 4 Skool*. It was an eye-opening experience for many people and it started a new musical pathway for the Korean Wave. BTS not only opened up a new pathway for the South Korean music industry, but had also ushered in a new age for global pop music.

●

Rehearsal studios instead of school
I danced and sang all night long
While you're playing, I perform my dreams
I held back sleep to hold my pen every night
Only to close my eyes after the sunrise

2 Cool 4 Skool
Track 2 "We Are Bulletproof Pt.2"
Released in June 2013

This song tells the story of the lives of the seven members; of how they struggled and endured as trainees to fulfill their dreams and reach for success. This is what caught my attention. I was overpowered by their honesty, down-to-the-point perspective, and most of all, the irresistible hip hop style and swagger.

Outro: "Circle Room Cypher"

Suga starts his rap:

●

My name is S-U-G-A
Other rappers are all behind me
As always with the cool beat
This way and that way
My tongue moves around
All your rap makes me sleepy
Shall we rewind this CD
Our music makes

The ladies cry
Our name is Bangtan
What's coming out of your mouth
Right now is Gamtan[admiration]

Then, continues RM:

●

But my voice is low
You are il-tan[version one] and I am sa-tan[version four]
I am Yi-ga-tan[Korean medicine] that heals you

Next is J-Hope:

●

Ma-ma-ma-ma-My name J-Hope
I don't leave a trace 'cause I'm so cool, like that pose
God damn, I'm the hip hop that
Gwangju gave birth to [J-Hope's home town]
This is the beginning of the Jeolla-do [province] rap
Shake you all up 'til you go bust
We're absolutely awesome

2 Cool 4 Skool
Track 7 "Circle Room Cypher"
Released in June 2013

After everyone had their turn, Jimin finally grabs the microphone and starts to rap. To me he sounds pretty good, but the other members jump in and jokingly yell out, "What are you doing, you should just leave." Then someone else says, "Let's go eat." Another member chimes in, "I'll treat you all," and another exclaims, "I'm out of here." After more chattering between the members, the track ends with the sound of a door closing.

Hidden track
Skit: On the Start Line

"On the Start Line" is a instrumental track with RM's narration.

●

Ah-ah (mic testing)

Trainee

In some ways, it defines me

But there's also no way to describe such a word

Don't belong anywhere

Not doing anything

That kind of period of transition

The most frustrating part of having the trainee status

Was being asked by friends and relatives

When can we see you [perform]?

When will you debut?

Those kinds of questions

I could not answer

Because I didn't know

I didn't have the answers either

Came here with confidence and self-belief

Awaiting here was a truly different reality

Even now after three years have passed

I could conquer the music industry

I can do it, so I believe until

I am told otherwise by the producers and trainers

Then I feel I am nothing

No more than a speck of dust

As if I am standing in front of the blue ocean

Only to turn around and face the desolate desert

With that kind of feeling really

Feeling like an hourglass

Spent three years as a trainee

And now I am finally about to debut

After my debut

There will be other oceans and other deserts waiting for me

I am not afraid, not even a bit

What made me today was

The ocean and desert that I have seen

I would never forget

That ocean and that desert

Because I am a trainee

2 Cool 4 Skool

Hidden Track 8 "On the Start Line"

Released in June 2013

Hidden track
Gil (Road/Path)

In this 9th Hidden track, I was most touched by these phrases:

●

Lots of pain and wounds... Brighten up the stars in my heart...
When you become weary, more stars would shine inside your heart.
No barefoot
Let's move forward
Wearing the shoes called Bangtan

To me, these were the most impressive lines in the track. It reminded me of the memoir *Wind, Sand, and Stars* by French author, Antoine-
Marie-Roger de Saint-Exupéry. Two pilots, who survived a plane crash
in the middle of the desert, are desperately walking to be saved by the
Bedouins, a nomadic group of Arab people. They walked and walked
without stopping. They chased a mirage and almost died but could not
stop walking. That, to me, is the essence of life.

BTS

Chapter 3

Hit-Man Si-Hyuk Bang
Creator of BTS

"Music is my life,
I am my music, and
Music is me."
Latin quote by unknown author

I opened the Korea Music Copyright Association site and punched in the name, Si Hyuk Bang, in the search box. A total of 651 songs were registered to that name as of April 21st, 2018. BTS' "DNA" lists the names of the people who participated in creating the music and the lyrics: Supreme Boi, RM, Woo-Ram Kim, Suga, Hitman Bang, Pdogg.

On the site, producer and composer, Bang is listed as 'Hitman Bang'. The word 'hit' follows him around as he creates and produces hit songs such as, "Like Being Shot by a Bullet" (Ji-Young Baek), "Bad Guy" (Rain), "I Fell in Love" (Ji-Yoon Park), "Without a Heart" (8eight), "Never Let You Go" (2AM), "Friday Night" (G.O.D). I browsed through the Internet to find new postings that were either by or about Bang, but I could not find any. I was hoping for some personal notes from the CEO of Big Hit Entertainment that would shed some light on his personality, style, and/or musical directions. However, I ended up having to use many different resources to write about the man who is like a 'father figure' to BTS.

"I'm not saying I'm gonna change the world, but I guarantee that I will spark the brain that will change the world."

Tupac Shakur
(1971–1996, Rapper, Actor, Poet, and the 'King of West Coast Hip Hop')

On December 11th, 2017, Bang had an interview as the producer of BTS with a journalist from The Segye Times.

Question: How do you feel about the fact that BTS aren't boys anymore? (Referring to their name Bangtan Boys)

Bang: Suga once told me he didn't want to be an adult. He wasn't referring to how Peter Pan always says he doesn't want to grow up. His explanation goes like this: Even when you become an adult, as long as you don't lose your dreams and keep going towards your goals, this makes you a boy and not an adult. I think this statement best describes BTS. When we were planning The Most Beautiful Moment in Life series, those words [of Suga] had a big influence on me.

The interview continued.

Question: Was BTS created to target the International market?

Bang: Many factors played a role for BTS to be in their current position. When we first created BTS, our main goal for the team was to 'maintain the true values of K-Pop.' As time went by, we began adding the 'values that are unique to BTS', the essence of what fans worldwide love and enjoy about BTS' music, to the existing values of K-Pop.

The True Values of K-Pop

What are the true values of K-Pop? The answer may vary depending on one's standpoint, as well as their musical and cultural background. K-Pop has evolved in many ways since the beginning of the first wave of 'Idol culture' that swept over South Korea during the mid-1990s. Since then, people started to identify Korean pop music as a total package that comes with stage performances highlighted by impeccably choreographed dance routines and an emphasis on captivating visuals. When Bang created BTS, he said that the one thing he wanted to protect was the true values of K-Pop. He believed that the music, visuals, and performances that adhered to the true values of K-Pop would be the critical factor required to overcome the language barriers between K-Pop and non-Korean speaking/international fans across the world.

•

Everyone around said don't overdo it
Going wild for music will only ruin your family

I just live by my own conviction
The way I want

Should ask those who prayed for my failure
Does it look like I ruined my family, punk?

The Most Beautiful Moment in Life Pt. 2,
Track 1 "Intro: Never Mind"
Released in November 2015

What did Bang mean when he mentioned the 'values that only belong to BTS'? What are the values of BTS? What makes them worthy? The first value I would like to talk about is their special individuality or 'non -substitutable personality.'

Bang had advised the members of BTS to write their own lyrics in order to bring out their unique, individual personalities. He asked them to write original lines and rejected anything that sounded too common, too mechanical, or lacking in sensitivity and emotions. For BTS, Bang did not want the kind of lyrics that anyone else could write. Soon enough, the boys began to produce the kind of lyrics Bang had been waiting for. Powerful and sharp, yet warm and dynamic; their voices and their stories began to shape BTS' unique sound. The members of BTS wrote freely and openly about their own lives; stories of their youth, of their desires, hopes, and dreams. They also learned how to incorporate social issues into their own stories and figured out how to deliver their messages to their fans, so they could share more ideas and feelings with the world.

The second value that I found unique to BTS is their conscientiousness. The members often talk about finding their identity and a desire to 'reach out to as many people as possible' with their music to 'change the world for the better.' The Chinese philosopher, Confucius, once said, "To put the world in order, we must first put the nation in order; to put the nation in order, we must first put the family in order; to put the family in order, we must first cultivate our personal life; we must first set our hearts right. "It took self-cultivation for the seven boys, during their trainee days, to prepare themselves to become who they are today - BTS. When their first album was released, they had grown into a seven-member family, which coincides with Confucius' teaching of 'putting the family in order'. With *"The Most Beautiful Moment in Life"* and change to *The Most Beautiful Moment in Life* album series, BTS 'put the nation in order'. Finally, they moved on to 'put the world in order' with *Wings and Love Yourself: Her* in 2017.

Love Yourself: Her was released on September 18th, 2017 at 6:00 PM PST (Korean time/GMT+9). By 8:00 am the next day, the 19th, the EP became the top-selling album in over seventy countries around the world: United States, United Kingdom, Australia, Canada, Belgium, Austria, Denmark, Finland, France, Germany, Greece, Luxemburg, Mexico, Netherlands, New Zealand, Norway, Portugal, Spain, Sweden, Switzerland,

Bulgaria, the Czech Republic, Estonia, Hungary, Latvia, Poland, Romania, Lithuania, Slovakia, Slovenia, Argentina, Brazil, Chile, Columbia, Costa Rica, Ecuador, El Salvador, Nicaragua, Peru, Brunei, Cambodia, Hong Kong, Laos, Macau, Malaysia, Philippines, Singapore, Taiwan, Thailand, Vietnam, Armenia, Azerbaijan, Belarus, India, Indonesia, Israel, Kazakhstan, Russia, South Africa, Turkey, Bangladesh, Corte d'Ivoire, Cameroon, Ethiopia, Libya, Liechtenstein, Maldives, Myanmar, Palestine, Ukraine, Japan, Mauritius.

The lead single "DNA" topped the Global iTunes Top Songs Chart and hit the number one spot on the popular songs chart in twenty some countries: Norway, Sweden, Bulgaria, Estonia, Hungary, Lithuania, Poland, Romania, Slovenia, Argentina, Brazil, Chile, El Salvador, Guatemala, Peru, Brunei, Hong Kong, Laos, Malaysia, Philippines, Singapore, Taiwan, Thailand, Vietnam, Belize, Indonesia, Kazakhstan, Turkey, and Ukraine. "DNA" also made BTS the highest-ranking K-Pop artist on the US iTunes Top Songs chart at number four. Their previous record was number eight with "Spring Day", the first single from the repackaged album of *Wings* released in 2017.

The third value of BTS can be summed up in this sentence: "We're able to be here because of the ARMYs. Thank you! We love you!" BTS said this after their historical live performance of "DNA" at the American Music Awards on November 19th, 2017. BTS is the first K-Pop artist to perform on stage at the AMAs, and that evening was also their first TV debut in the U.S. RM recalled that night as an exciting, but nervous experience. He comments, "I couldn't hear anything on stage, and I just couldn't believe [we were there]. Lots of artists wanted to do a collaboration with us. Zedd said we should get together sometime. You don't know what'll come out of it, but I hope it works out." Zedd is a Russian-German musician, record producer, and songwriter. He has had quite a successful career with hit songs like "Clarity" featuring Foxes (peaked at number eight on the Billboard Hot 100) and "Stay" with Alessia Cara (peaked at number seven on the Billboard Hot 100 Chart). He was also featured on Ariana Grande's "Break Free" (peaked at number four on the Billboard Hot 100 Chart).

At the AMAs, Jungkook was full of confidence. He said, "It was such a prestigious event. We were extremely tense, but our fans chanted very loudly and that made us relax. We would love to come back next year." The following year, 2018, they made history once again at the Billboard Music Awards by being named as the Top Social Artist for the second consecutive year and performed their new single "Fake Love" for the first time for the US fans. "Fake Love" was released in May, but Amazon started the pre-sale on April 18th, 2018. The album quickly rose to become a best seller on Amazon.

The Top Social Artist Award was expected by a lot of people. The Billboard Music Awards had already seen and experienced BTS' popularity. Their social media ads aired previews of BTS with phrases like, "You can see BTS at the BBMAs. ARMY, aren't you excited?" Introducing a new album or song at the Billboard Music Awards with millions of viewers watching is not the usual way for Korean artists, or any other artists for that matter, to debut their new content. While most K-Pop stars would do what is known as a Comeback Special on major TV music programs, BTS performed their new song "Fake Love" on the stage of the Billboard Music Awards on May 20th, 2018. With this performance, they also kicked off the release of their third studio album *Love Yourself: Tear*.

Going back to the night of the AMAs, Suga was feeling surreal saying, "I was so nervous to be on the stage. I grew up watching [the

AMAs]. I had never been so nervous before. I still can't believe we were on stage [at the AMAs]." RM's interview after the AMAs continued, "I can't say I'm fully satisfied with our performance tonight, but I'm glad we went on the stage at the AMAs and made ourselves known. All the participating artists talked about us. They all said our fans were great." J-Hope, V, and Jin also mentioned their fans. "We were there because of ARMYs." BTS never fails to express appreciation for their fans. It is those humble and kind words and attitude that show how special and humane these boys are. Confucius once said, "Music is courtesy." If that's the case, the most courteous boy group, BTS, must be music itself.

PART

2

I have an eating disorder
No matter what I eat
Always hungry for you

Impossible to describe
A girl like you
It goes beyond the poetic license

Good house, good car
Those things can't be happiness
Still I want to give them to you

Skool Luv Affair
Track 1 "Intro: Skool Luv Affair"
Released in February 2014

Chapter 4

2017 American Music Awards
DNA Live Performance

When I look back and piece together everyone's opinions (from both BTS and the fans), there was, in fact, a turning point when everything started to change for BTS. It was the song "Dope". It first drew responses from people doing reaction videos on YouTube—this is where the international fan base began to form. According to Korean fandom terminology, they started 'business', so to speak. The international fan base then exploded with "Fire" and continued to expand with "Blood Sweat & Tears", the latter song has a much wider appeal to general audiences when compared to BTS' previous songs. The American press started to recognize [BTS] with their presence on Billboard and the AMAs. After that, it snowballed and now we have BTS as we know them today.

Si-Hyuk Bang (CEO, Big Hit Entertainment)

Words could not describe the overwhelming atmosphere inside the Microsoft Theatre when BTS' silhouettes appeared with white backlighting on the sea blue stage. The audience screamed, cried, chanted in both English and Korean, and followed the dance moves as BTS performed "DNA". The seven members totally stole the show that evening at the 45th American Music Awards. The audience watched them in awe as they realized BTS were not just another K-Pop boy group. As the audiences raised their arms and began to move their bodies, they almost looked like angels to my eyes. Many people began taking out their smart phones to capture every single moment of that performance. With their sincere lyrics and powerful performances, BTS was speaking through their music; telling their own story and making history.

●

Since the day the universe was created
Beyond the infinite worlds
In our previous life and perhaps in our next life
We'll be together forever

All this is no coincidence
Because we've found our destiny
DNA

Love yourself: Her
Track 2 "DNA"
Released in September 2017

The Most Beautiful Moment in Life
The Third Extended Play

When I bought the album *The Most Beautiful Moment in Life*, I handled it as if it was like treasure and couldn't remove the vinyl immediately. After waiting a bit, I peeled open the vinyl cover slowly with caution and in the end, I couldn't bring myself to throw away the vinyl cover so I ended up keeping it.

Baby pink, or apricot? A faded flower petal? A soft-feathered bird? The color and the texture of the album jacket reminded me of many things, but that's not all—there was something strange. I heard something from the album that I was holding. How come? I wondered how it's possible for me to hear a noise when I have not even played it. I stared at the album and I saw flower petals dancing in my mind's eye. There was a spring breeze outside the window which shook the windowsills. I finally removed the entire vinyl cover including the sticker that said, 'Hot Tracks / 16,500 won'.

I looked at the title, 'Hwa-Yang-Yeon-Hwa' (花樣年華), which in Chinese letters means 'Flower-Shape-Year-Shiny'. This phrase roughly translates to mean "The Most Beautiful Moment in Life." I opened the album and found a small booklet of 120 pages. It had lots of images and pictures while also including eight blank pages, four memo pages, four pages of blank sheet music, and ten pages of lyrics. All seven members had left personal notes after they finished recording the album—those notes added up to seven pages. I started to look at the photos and saw that the members of BTS were photographed in short-sleeved shirts in an open field full of yellow flowers. The images looked almost dreamlike. It could have been spring or early summer since in one of the photos, the boys were on a cherry blossom tree. In other photos, they were standing in front of a pond with the cherry blossoms in full bloom. While they see-

med exhausted by their own beauty, they still look enraptured and focused in the moment.

I continued flipping the pages and moved on to look at the studio shots. They were drinking water, looking at flowers, leaning by the window, and laying down on a sofa. In a few other shots they were sitting in a bathtub fully dressed and drawing with their fingers on steamed windows. The pictures got more and more vibrant as I turned the pages; it was a fine photo album.

I finally played the CD and paid attention to the first track.

Intro: The Most Beautiful Moment in Life

●

The rim looks more distant today
On the court, I let out a sigh
A boy who fears reality
When he shoot the ball
That's the only time he's at ease
He throws the ball by himself
What I throw at the rim
Numerous worries and life's troubles
I act as if I know the world
But my body is not ready

In this track I sensed a fusion of Eminem's style of hip hop and James Brown's style of funk. The 'body' that's 'not ready' reminded me of my youth when I would deliberately wrinkle my school uniform and cock the school uniform hat sideways to look cool. I wanted to ditch all my classes, especially on warm days when the smell of the lilacs and the acacia trees wafted through the open windows. I remember feeling flustered and wanting to open the pages of real life rather than the textbooks.

'Rim' is a metaphor for success, applause, acclamation, popularity, honor, and boastfulness; the sense of leaving a loser's life and entering a lavish one. When the ball goes into the rim, you will find happiness.

●

Laughter leaves me along with the ball
Breath rising to my chin
Squirming dreams
Faster dribble, my heart gets happier
I feel like this moment may last forever
But when the night falls again
Reality gets destroyed
When I come around, I get scared again like an idiot

Success was only a symbol—it wasn't a fact or reality. When the night comes, the fool returns even more scared than ever before.

●

Breathe, breathe
Or dream
Row again right now
Along with your heartbeat

This is the main message of the song: breathe or dream. BTS are telling all the young people to choose between those two actions. Either breathe or dream but go forward with your own heartbeat.

The Most Beautiful Moment in Life pt. 1
Track 1 "Intro: The Most Beautiful Moment in Life"
Released in April 2015

Chapter 5

Love Yourself: Her

Intro: Serendipity

●

All this is no coincidence
Just, just with my feelings
Whole world is different from yesterday
Just, just with your happiness
You called me, and I was your flower
Like we've been waiting we bloomed and dazzled
Perhaps nature's course that's all there was
You know, I know
You are me, I am you

You are my green mold
My angel who saved me, my world
I am your tri-colored cat
That has come to meet you
Love me now
Touch me now
Just let me love you
Just let me love you
All was decided from the beginning of time
Just let me love you
Let me love you

Love Yourself: Her
Track 1 "Intro: Serendipity"
Released in September 2017

This song talks about the joyous event of finding that special some-one. BTS is certain that this does not happen by chance, but that love is predestined as part of a natural chain of events. The track bumps with a mixture of R&B and pop.

DNA

At last, I play "DNA" and feel the strong beat—the song speaks to something deep in my soul. BTS' lyrics and melody seem to leave the earth's atmosphere and travel to the outer reaches of the universe. An unfamiliar sensation fills my heart. At first, it seems like the feeling of being impressed, but no, it's something much more than just an appreciation for talent. Fullness may be the right word to describe my feeling when listening to "DNA"—it's as if the song's beat is harmoniously playing along with the beat in my heart. It's something akin to an out-of-body experience, as if my mind and soul are separating from the physical world. A sensa-tion in my heart begins to build—it's an overwhelming feeling that makes my heart feel as if it might burst from my chest. "DNA" is like another source of light, something like a second sun. Its bright existence engulfs those who listen to it in warmth that's both comforting and exciting; fresh and exhilarating.

●

Don't look back
We found our destiny
Don't regret it, baby
Forever
Forever
We're together

Love Yourself: Her
Track 2 "DNA"
Released in September 2017

Best of Me

"Best of Me" presents itself as a mix of happy and sad feelings that are almost bittersweet. It's as if I can feel the pain and the bitterness of the tears of the boys as they start vocalizing the lyrics. As the song escalates, the voices begin panting with restrained passion; the voice gradually increases in urgency and tempo until they finally crescendo into an explosion of vocal fireworks that fade slowly into the darkness. Interesting parallels can be drawn between this crescendo of music and the important things in life—the most genuine moments and feelings are usually the most fleeting and ephemeral. BTS proves again that they can leverage their unique sound to inspire feelings like those experienced during the happiest moments in life. All-the-while, their music persists as a reminder that the reality of happiness is that it is fleeting and should be cherished as such—it is a kind of musical artistry that only BTS can achieve.

●

When you say that you love me
I am walking in the sky
Tell me about eternity, just one more time
When you say that you love me
That's all I need to hear
That you won't change, just one more time

To me you are
Everyday
Summer and winter

So please don't leave me
You got the best of me

Love Yourself: Her
Track 3 "Best of Me"
Released in September 2017

At the end of this track, I feel as if I have just finished the most satisfying meal. Like a truly balanced perfect meal, BTS chose the perfect individual elements to make up this perfect meal of a track. All the essential ingredients were present: peace, love, freedom, and happiness which all intertwined to create a singular 'love confession'. Each element of the song comes together to create something greater than the sum of its parts, the same way that a chef might orchestrate a meal to create an experience more powerful than any individual ingredient.

Dimples

This track encompasses the very definition of "cute", and it speaks to the inborn human desire for all things charming and adorable. Everyone acts the same way when they fall in love. Love makes people do silly things that others can't understand. At the same time, people in love will believe that they are acting normally; this is the essence of what makes people in love cute. "Dimples" epitomizes this cuteness and is a symbol for this seemingly paradoxical duality of love.

Simply put, this song is about someone with dimples. She gets dimples when she smiles. He thinks her dimples are perfect and beautiful like an angel or a rainbow, but he can't get close to her dimples. The song "Dimples" describes her dimples as being cruel because he can't see them whenever he wants to. She might not have intended for her dimples to be so cruel, but to him they are cruel dimples. He wants to see them closer but can't think of a way. Out of this dilemma a song is born. When you get lost and can't find the way, sometimes composing a song is your only recourse.

●

You hidden yet only appear when you smile
Where did you come from?
Don't tell a lie, you are an angel
What exactly are you
But you, your smile is cruel
Cruel, I shouldn't have laid my eyes on your cheeks
You, But what's really dangerous
Only is in your posession

Those dimples, illegal
No, it's dangerous, oh yes
So, I call you ille-girl
Your existence alone is illegal
Were you a mistake that an angel left behind

Or a deep kiss
Those dimples are illegal
But I want it anyway, anyway, anyway

Love Yourself: Her
Track 4 "Dimples"
Released in September 2017

Skit: Billboard Music Awards Speech

The Billboard Music Awards was the event that proved BTS's global presence. Upon accepting the Top Social Artist award, RM expressed
appreciation to the fans worldwide. "ARMY, our fandom, thank you very
much. And, you know we still cannot believe that we're standing here on
the stage of the Billboard Music Awards, oh my gosh, and it is so great
to see all the artists we admire and feel honored to be in this category
with such great artists, you know, like, right in front of us. It's really an
honor and most importantly this award belongs to every... people all
around the world that shine the love and light on us by the millions and
make BTS really proud everywhere. Please, ARMY, remember what we
say: love yourself." He then continued in Korean, "We really love you and
thank you. We, BTS, will try to be better." He concluded with another
thank you, "Thank you Billboard for supporting us. Thank you!"

It was an amazing speech that reminded me of an old Italian saying:
"When you have something to be thankful for, engrave it on the marble;
when you have done a favor for someone, let it flow down the river." RM's
statement represents an engraving of BTS' thankful minds; words per-
manently etched into history as a token of BTS' gratitude towards their
fans.

BTS is never arrogant, conceited, or overconfident. Some famous
stars try to be mysterious and hide themselves from their fans, but these
boys have consistently shown that they are open and humble. They go

on social media and communicate with their fans. They also upload rehearsal videos for the whole world to see who they are and what they do.
They try to reach out to the world and everyone who is willing to listen.
The message they're trying so very hard to convey is this: love yourself.
In a sense, it has the same meaning as Socrates' 'know yourself'. Socrates
believed that one cannot begin to understand others and the complex
world around them unless they understand their own self, first and fore-
most. BTS asks everyone to look inwards to see what they are truly see-
king. Only then can they move on to know and realize that dream. In the
same way the boys have discovered themselves, they want their fans to
know themselves, love themselves, and to follow their own dreams.

MIC Drop

"MIC DROP" is a revenge song for all the haters who have put down BTS
out of jealousy and envy.

●

Mic mic bungee
Bright light, proceed
You thought I was gonna mess it up
I'm fine, sorry
Sorry "Billboard"
Sorry "worldwide"
Sorry mom, your son is too hot
Do hyodo[taking care of one's parents] on your behalf
Absolutely no podo [grapes - sold out] at our concert

I do it I do it, you're a bad ratatouille

Sue me if you get sick

Sue it

Did you see my bag

Did you see my bag

A bag full of trophies

How you think bout that

How you think bout that

Haters are giving up already

My success is already golden

I'm so firin' firin' like a torchbearer

You're rushin' rushin' to run away

How you dare

How you dare

How you dare

Too many trophies in my hands

Too heavy, my two hands aren't enough

MIC Drop

MIC Drop

f-f-feet, careful with your feet

w-w-words, careful with your words

Haters gon' hate
Players gon' play
Live a life, man
Good luck

No need to see you again, my last good-bye
Nothing more to say, don't even apologize

Watch closely, you'll end up just the same
We shoot up like Coca-Cola
Your corneas will be in such a shock
p-p-pretty cool, c-c-cool

Love Yourself: Her
Track 7 "MIC DROP"
Released in September 2017

The term 'mic drop' is generally used to describe a gesture in which a performer or speaker drops or throws the microphone down to the floor after they have a successful performance or speech. BTS' "MIC DROP" is a message of triumph against their haters. No matter who criticizes them, their bag is 'full of trophies', their concert tickets are sold out, they are the center of attention, and they are the center of the world's music business. They don't worry about their future anymore. Instead, they ask questions like, "Which country are we going to next," "How long is the flight," "What is the local time," and occasionally get upset over "a steak that's not cooked right to their liking." This mention of a steak reminds me of a story about Frank Sinatra and a hotel in Australia. Sinatra was upset with the rude hotel staff, so he purchased the hotel next day—it's what some stars do. I think stars today are treated like Greek gods. They

can do anything and get away with it. BTS has obtained that special star status, but the boys seem level-headed and never overdo it.

Go Go

The original Korean title of the song is "Instead of Worrying, Go." It starts with a Rumba rhythm which makes me think that BTS should collaborate with the world-famous guitarist Carlos Santana someday. They begin to spit out sounds and shout as if they're going to pass out. They are relaxed, free, and delighted as if today is the last day of their lives and this album is the last album they will ever record. Like General Yi Soon-Shin's famous words, "If you try to hold on to your life, you will end up dead; if you're determined to fight until death, you will live." That's the secret of life, and BTS understood this.

●

I want cruisin' on the bay
Want cruisin' like NEMO
No money but want to go somewhere far away
Don't have money but want to rest up
Have no money but want some Jiro Ono [Japanese sushi chef]

Worked so hard to earn my pay
Spend it all on my stomach
Pinching pennies to spend it all on wasting it
Let me be,
Even if i'm overspending
Even if I withdraw all my savings tomorrow

Like a crazy guy

Woo there's no tomorrow
There's already a mortgage on my future
Woo, spending more of my money
Friends, wassup
Do you want some?

Just break it apart
We're too young to just worry
Today instead of worrying, Go

Instead of worrying, Go
Instead of worrying, Go

Love Yourself: Her
Track 8 "Go Go"
Released in September 2017

This song incorporates the poetic spirit of the pastoral sound of Scottish bagpipes. It is also mixed with the sensation of the sounds of South America—there is special emphasis on the sound of the pan flute from Peru. "Go Go" tells a story of a young man with very little income who doesn't have much money saved up. He loses his temper in the moment, and he suddenly withdraws all his money from the bank and spends it. He wastes everything he has, but BTS isn't pointing fingers. They wouldn't call the young man a loser, but instead they try to rationalize the man's action and want to console him. "We're too young to worry, instead of worrying, go."

Outro: Her

"Outro: Her" describes a person who is longing to find himself. While he is happy to be in love, to be in a state where there's only 'she' in his life and only 'he' in her life, he feels that he has lost himself. Even if the universe had disappeared, only their love would remain. The question this track poses is whether this kind of love is sustainable. Is it possible to have love like this and survive in the real world?

Author of *The Little Prince*, Antoine de Saint-Exupery states that "love is not looking at each other, but looking together in the same direction." In "Outro: Her", the singer wants the kind of love in which he can hold hands with his beloved and watch the sunset together. However, he also wants to find himself, see the world, and spend time with his own friends. He needs his own private moments, but she wants him all the time. She expects him to be with her and only love her always.

●

Anyway, I want to be the best man for you
Perhaps it's natural since you're the world to me
When you said you wanted to die with me
I promised to be what you wanted me to be
God, I swore to myself

Maybe I am your truth and lie
Maybe I am your love and hate
Maybe I am your enemy and friend
Your heaven and hell, your pride and shame
I could never remove the mask

I am not the one you know underneath it
As always make up to wake up
And dress up to mask on

You're the answer to all of my wonder
I call you her, her
Because you're my tear, tear

The girl he loves, he can only love her so much. She is his sun and he can't live without her light and heat. At the same time, he can also melt and die like Icarus who flew too close to the sun. That's why he sometimes avoids her. It's also why it's perfectly okay for him even if 'she was a fake' if 'she holds' him. Because she was his 'beginning and end', he also tries to be the one that she loves with the mask on.

●

As always mask on
Welcoming me with a cheer, her
I'm your star, shining as if nothing is wrong
But when I shine the most, I take the mask off
Lost star, I put down my load, enjoying the darkness
No lights to shot me down as to kill me
I just go where my heart takes me
Do as I feel like, nothing holds me down
Tick tock the dark is over
Again, to be your best
I get a hold of myself

Love makes one go crazy

Yeah, this is a crazy man's determination

Apply to the formula that fits me best

Give you an answer, I concluded for you

who is everything

But you love that

That makes me try more

I find new meaning because of you,

And so the night shines

I know, even after the darkness

To me you're the morning

You woke me up

Love Yourself: Her
Track 9 "Outro: Her"
Released in September 2017

Hidden Track 1

Skit: Hesitation and Fear

The first hidden track starts 29 seconds after the 9th track, "Outro: Her", ends. The members drop in on Si-Hyuk Bang's studio. It is a surprise visit for Bang who was watching the Billboard Music Awards alone. He is flustered for being caught off guard, and the boys wouldn't let a fun chance like this slip away. They start teasing their producer:

"Oh, what were you watching, Mr. Producer?"

"How are you doing? Oh, isn't this the BMA show?"

"Are you watching it again? Are you going to be joining ARMY?"

"Don't be embarrassed, it's understandable."

"When was that? May? It's been over three months."

The recording captured their conversation and laughter thoroughly. It also reveals something they never talked about at interviews and TV appearances. In 2010, when they were trainees, they didn't know anything about the Billboard charts. Someone says that he didn't even know that the Grammy Awards had anything to do with music. He had thought 'Grammy' was just some girl's name. But who cares? The whole world had seen them at the Billboard Music Awards in 2017 and 2018.

They move on to talk about different things.
"In ten years, we may be doing solo activities…"

They think about their future. They consider how the group could evolve or change and how that will affect each member's career.

"This may be the highest point we're able to reach in our career. It was so hard for us to get here, but the downhill can happen overnight. Going down is always faster than climbing up."

"But we've grown so much. Remember when we used to go to the convenient store and eat that hot dog snack? Those 1,300 won ($1.15) or 1,500 won ($1.30) hot dogs tasted so good."

"Yeah, back then Namjoon used to give us advice at that place under the Jam-Shil Bridge."

"Oh, I got it at a café."

"I thought we were going to be really bad. I'm still nervous about all our success. It gives me anxiety. Going down will be faster than climbing up."

"Wasn't Billboard like meeting someone new for the first time, like a first date?"

"Sing something."

"What was Jimin's song that he practiced during his lessons? 'Why call me' from a 1975 movie?"

"Sometimes I feel as if we're acting."

"It's hard, but it's not acting. We're just being presented nicely like a well-wrapped present."

And they keep on going with their usual conversation…

Ocean

Peaceful voices tell a story of BTS facing the ocean. A fierce and harsh ocean that has water which bites like the winter chills. Standing before the blue waves, BTS see a desert. They're throwing away all their achievements because they are things of the past. You need a new achievement for today. Relying on past achievements is the same as walking into a coffin and closing the cover. The past is dead and relying on it will cause you to lose all vital power and you'll eventually become something akin to a zombie or vampire.

I find this hidden track as valuable as the story of King Midas. When King Midas picked up a piece of bread, it turned to gold. When he touched his beloved daughter, she turned into gold. King Midas eventually died surrounded by gold. However, for BTS, it won't be gold they turn everything into but peace and love through passion and dance. This 11th track symbolizes our society where gold is everything and where it seems like only those with money can survive and thrive.

We have to surrender all hope
For all the hardships

BTS throw themselves into despair so that they can endure and overcome hardships. They would rather walk a thorny path, but that same path will turn into a field of roses in the future. They write, sing, practice, rehearse, and do concerts day and night. They travel around the world to reach out to people. Their goal is to share their love with youth all around the world so that others can be empowered to follow their dreams and make this world a better place.

And they're not ready to stop.

Don't want to rest

That voice is a voice of hope and love for dreams; a dream from the boys' hearts. Their conclusion is, "We are love".

BTS' way of love means learning how to, "surrender all hope" in order to "overcome hardships". You have to take a step into the entrance of despair, so that you can gain the strength to overcome and reach the road to love and freedom.

BTS sets sail on another ship traveling the sea of despair, also known as this world. They are in search for an island called hope. They know the voyage won't be easy, but they are ready for all the challenges it will bring.

Where there is hope
There is always hardship

They know they must choose hardships. They don't get distracted by traps. They march through the hardships like warriors, and at the end, they reach the light, the flowers, and the stars.

●

Reached the ocean accidentally
I look at the beach
Countless grains of sand
Fierce and harsh wind
I still see a desert
Drank all of you 'cause I wanted to have the ocean
But thirstier than before
What I know, is it really ocean
Or is it a blue desert

I don't know I don't know
If I'm feeling the waves yeah
I don't know I don't know
If I'm still being chased by the sand storm yeah
I don't know I don't know
Whether it is the ocean, or the desert,
Or hope, or despair
Real or fake shit

Love Yourself: Her
Track 11 (Hidden) "Ocean"
Released in September 2017

PART

3

If I get first place,

Does that make me a successful artist?

That's good too, but…I wanna do music

I'll just do what I want for now

So just leave me alone

From the Album, DARK&WILD
TRACK 13 "2nd Grade"

BTS "Thanks To" from their Second Korean Studio Album *WINGS*

On April 30th, 2018 at 11:43 AM, when I visited the official online fan cafe for BTS (Daum Bangtan Fan Cafe), this cafe was a place for 1,058,962 fans, and counting, to communicate with one another and share their love for BTS.

Excerpt from RM's "Thanks To"

'My beloved parents, sister, and Mon! I love you. Grandfather, grandmother, and my maternal grandfather who are in Heaven, I love you. Maternal grandmother, please stay healthy. I'll come visit you. My dear relatives, thank you.

Producer Bang, Vice-president Yoojung, Director Shinkyu, Director Seok-joon, Director Hyuk, and Director Chaeeun thank you.'

This is how RM's "Thanks To" begins, followed by many people's names. With his statement of 'Big Hit is the best company', it makes one assume that the company's working environment must be somewhat harmonious. Of course, this is not the end of it. Many more names follow his "Thanks To" list as he states, 'Special thanks to Gaeko, and my precious couple of friends. You guys are that much more precious because there are only a few of you. I miss you a lot.'

Being a friend of RM, the leader of BTS, doesn't sound so bad at all.

RM also brings up 'All the staff members that help us, whom I don't really remember their faces and names,' Now that BTS has become a world-renowned boy group, they must have a lot of staff helping them to run their schedules smoothly. Naturally, it would be difficult to remember all those faces and names.

In the late 90s, I conducted an interview with Woo-Hyuk Jang from H.O.T. Woo-Hyuk told me that when they release an album, they promote the album for two months before they go on a hiatus to prepare for their next album—this essentially keeps them busy 24/7. They said they didn't even have the time to eat during those two months promoting their album. I asked, "You guys have a couple of managers, can't you just stop by a 24-hour convenience store to buy a rice ball or something?" Woo-Hyuk shook his head no and said, "We don't have that time." This says it all. No time to even stop by somewhere to grab a bite of food. On average, H.O.T had around ten scheduled events per day and returned to their dorms around 2 AM. Once they returned to their dorms, they headed straight to dance practice. Hearing this made me realize, "Wow, in the end,

it's all about putting in the effort. It's all about practicing. That is what decides whether you will accomplish your dream or not." Success and failure can both be in the palm of our hands, but without putting in your blood, sweat, and tears, that success will be out of reach.

Excerpt from SUGA's "Thanks To"

Suga's "Thanks To" begins with thanking the staff of Big Hit.

'To Big Hit's heart and soul, producer Si-Hyuk Bang, Big Hit's music team, Big Hit's feet—the manager team'

'Sunghyung-hyung, Hyunjoo-noona, Sunkyung-noona, and Gabriel-hyung who takes care of BTS' style, thank you'

'Choreographer Sungdeuk who doesn't need any explaining'

'Sunjung-noona, Mijung-noona, Yeonhee-nim, Seungwoo-nim, Hyunryung -nim, and Hyewon-nim from the artist development team—it would be hard to make a team like BTS again. Haha-haha'

'BTS's mental support Woojung-noona, Team leader Heesoon, who sacrifices a lot for our great performances, Yiseul-noona who takes care of Fan Marketing, Nayeob-noona, and Yuri-nim, I know you guys go through a lot'

'Style team's Department Head Jungsil'

'Department Head Naejoo and Dareum who gives us cool hairstyles and makeup'

'Director Lum, Director Hyunwoo, and Director Sungwoo who always create cool emotional music videos, thank you!'

Suga ends his "Thanks To" by thanking ARMY—'This 2nd full album is for you guys. Once again, thank you.'

Excerpt from JUNGKOOK's "Thanks To"

'My one and only family—mom, dad, and older brother, generally I might act indifferent, but please be understanding because I'm not actually like that on the inside. Even if I don't listen to you guys well I am still mom and dad's son. And Sergeant Jean... take it easy (Sergeant Jean is Jung Kook's older brother who was in the military)! I'm just kidding, you'll be discharged soon. Think about what you want to do when you get discharged from the military.'

Jungkook also thanks the staff at Big Hit Entertainment. I'll introduce a few.

'Director Chaeeun, your force is not a joke. Although we don't see each other often, thank you for giving me bread last time. I ate that bread deliciously.'

'Manager Hobum, who looks very tired these days, we need to have a meal together with all seven of us'

'Hayan-noona, who works so hard to the point where her dark circles come down to her chin! Thank you for your work, but hurry up and teach me English and Japanese! lol'

'Jinah-nim, Kyungjin-nim, Sungho-nim, Hyeyoung-nim, I don't really know

you but I know you guys are working hard for us and for the company! Fighting!'

Jungkook also thanks his bandmates. Rather than thanking them, this is more like giving them high-fives for coming this far and to tell them—let's do a good job going forward as well.

'I'm not sure if Bangtan hyungs will read this or not, but I'm writing this. I'm really glad we got to come this far together as a group. I believe we have seven heads, but one body (it sounds weird just imagining that). If we all look at different places, our body would not know what to do so let's all look at the same place and climb up as far as we can. You all know where that is.'

Now Jungkook thanks ARMY.

'Because you guys have given me so much love, I don't think there will be any love to receive if I am born again in the next life. I want to become someone's great person and your eternal singer. I can't bring myself to lose you guys. If you guys drift away, I will step closer to you guys. I don't know how I will do that and if it would work or not, but I will do my best to not let you guys go. Once again, thank you and I love you.'

This was Jungkook's "Thanks To", which was full of compassion.

Excerpt from J-HOPE's "Thanks To"

'This is our 2nd Full Album!!!!!! I am going to start writing down all the names of my people who I love the most and who I am most thankful to!!!!! (Caution, there's a lot)'

I will take him at his word and skip over to his words for BTS.

'And our members, you guys all know even if I don't say it right??? RM, Jin, Suga, Jimin, Tae-hyung, and Jungkook; everyone I know more than anyone, everyone I cherish more than anyone, and the people I love more than anyone, I love you guys until death. Now that we started this, let's fly all the way to the top!! Fighting, thank you!!!'

BTS
'Thanks To from DARK & WILD'

"I feel uncomfortable when people call me BTS' father. It's because artists aren't created by someone. From the moment I am called father or dad, BTS becomes an object and I become a creator. I feel uncomfort-

able because it doesn't align with my philosophy. Another thing is that I am not married, so when I'm called dad or father, my family at home has a hard time because everyone thinks I am married. Please save this bachelor (laughs). BTS members usually just call me PD-nim."

Si-Hyuk Bang

RM

'Bang Si-Hyuk PD-nim, thank you for letting the world know of our existence. BTS and ARMY, I love you guys and let's fly higher. Thank you. I love you.'

SUGA

'I love you BTS, and our forever companion ARMY who love us unconditionally!! Thank you so much. It's all thanks to you ARMY that we got to release our full album after a good year. You guys are ready to be with us for the next 10, 20 years, right? :) Saying I love you is not enough to express how I feel. I love you and Thank You.'

JIN

'Vice President Yoojung Choi who always take care of us… Woojung-noona who is busy taking care of us young kids… Yoonji-noona who turned out to be a master in Chinese, sorry I sneakily ate chips without letting you know… Sunkyung-nim who always come to work on-time… Half-angel, half-devil Eunhee-noona, Minkyung-noona who I can slowly see the devil in her… Soobin-noona who is very chic… and ARMY, thank you so much for always being there for us and I hope you guys stay as long as possible next to us! Lastly, I love you.'

J-HOPE

'My teachers and friends who always cheer us on from International High School in Gwangju… I always feel thankful… I would also like to thank all my other friends who cheer us on... Lastly, Destroymon, Shoop brother, Jjin brother, View, Jeon Jungguen, I love you and let's always be together. And to ARMY, I won't talk long—we are here because of you guys. I always love you, love you, and love you. Thank you.'

V

'Hello, this is the "Thanks To." (Bow) Thank you for opening this album... General Manager Yeonok who has a husband... Our ARMYs~ You've waited long huh~? Sorry. It took a while because we wanted to come back cooler than ever. Thank you so much I'll make it up to you. Although we only have the stage, we'll do our best every second of it~'

JIMIN

'I'll do my best to make BTS shine more... Hyungjoon-hyung, you don't get to sleep as much, Mika sensei please continue to teach me Japanese well. Thank you for the hard work... BTS I love you. ARMY thank you for believing in us and rooting for us whenever and wherever you are. We will also work hard and think about ARMY whenever and wherever, to show you guys great performances.'

JUNGKOOK

'The ACC staff members who help us out a lot with our Japanese promotions! Chorong-noona who helps us out with our International promotions! I'm always thankful! Lastly our ARMY I really love you all. RM, JIN, SUGA, J-HOPE, JIMIN, and V-hyung, I love you guys!'

If we take a look at BTS' "Thanks To", they always thank their family members first. This is followed by thanking Producer Si-Hyuk Bang and the staff members of Big Hit Entertainment. Finally, they thank their fans and fellow BTS members, promising to do their best on stage for great performances.

071

Chapter 6

2017, 2018 Billboard Music Award
BTS awarded the Top Social Artist award for 2 consecutive years

"Honestly, I'm not interested in national sports games. Ever since I was young, I've always wondered, 'Why are national events [such as the Olympics or the World Cup] such a big deal?'. Although I've heard BTS was doing well internationally, it didn't hit me until I saw their performance in person at the award show. It felt as if I had the Korean flag embroidered on the side of my chest; it was a touching moment. I felt that we need to do our best or else we'll become historical sinners (laughs)."

Bang Si-Hyuk (Songwriter, Lyricist)

In 2017, the Idol hip hop group BTS became the first ever K-Pop act to win the Top Social Artist award at the Billboard Music Awards, an award which honors the artist's social media presence. This was the second time a Korean singer won an award at the Billboard Music Awards. Korean singer PSY was the first Korean artist to win an award at the BMAs with the Top Streaming Song (Video) category with "Gangnam Style" in 2013.

The award show took place at the T-Mobile Arena in Las Vegas, Nevada on May 21st of 2017 at 5PM PST. The winner for the 'Top Social Artist' category was determined by taking into consideration various factors such as the amount of records sold/streamed, the number of times their songs were aired on the radio, fan engagement on social platforms, and fan votes online. The voting began on May 1st of 2017 on the Billboard website and the winner was chosen based on all the factors above.

The reason why BTS' win was so impressive was because the nominees included stars like Justin Bieber, Selena Gomez, Ariana Grande, and Shawn Mendes. During the acceptance speech, BTS' leader RM said, "We still cannot believe that we're standing here on the stage at the Billboard Music Awards. Most importantly this award belongs to every person all around the world that shines love and light on us by the millions and make BTS proud". RM made his speech in English and he also said in

Korean, "I really love you and thank you."

In 2018, BTS was awarded the Top Social Artist Award once again at the Billboard Music Awards.This made it their second consecutive win. On the day before the award show, Jimin interacted with ARMYs by doing a live social media broadcast through the app, V-live. Jimin's live broadcast began with four people watching. Viewership quickly grew into the thousands, and eventually it reached over 110,000 ARMYs watching from all around the world. Although he must have been tired after the rehearsals preparing for the award show, Jimin talked to the fans for over 20 minutes. One can't help but notice how much love he has for the fans and how sincere he is in his interactions with them.

The 2018 Billboard Music Awards was where BTS had their comeback performance, singing their latest song, "FAKE LOVE." A few things that stood out from the performance was how RM's rap was filled with confidence and Jungkook's abs were shown on stage. For BTS, this stage meant a lot to them because when they received the Top Social Artist award in 2017, they did not get to perform on stage. However, in 2018, it became a comeback stage for them where they received an award and got to perform in front of the audience—it's true when people say good things happen to those who wait. During the acceptance speech, RM states how they had a chance to think about what "social" really means for them with the consecutive win and how BTS realized their words carry a weight that impacts their fans. By ending the speech thanking the fans, it prominently shows how BTS and their fans are influenced by each other.

After the 2018 Billboard Music Awards, BTS did not attend the after party. It was a great opportunity to interact with world famous stars, but BTS politely declined and came back to their hotel room to have their own after party with their fans via a live broadcast. As always, BTS told their fans, "ARMYs, you've won the award!" as if BTS had accepted the award on behalf of the fans. On May 22nd, Jimin posted on BTS' official twitter account saying, "It was a really enjoyable and happy experience. I was nervous, so I don't think I got to say everything I wanted to. You guys won this award. I won't forget. I love you guys."

With more than 550,000 ARMYs attending, BTS' world tour concerts have grown to become a place where BTS and their fans discuss the prejudices in this world. BTS is constantly looking for ways their music can help overcome the oppression afflicting this generation by creating a new world filled with freedom, peace, and love. This is the reason why I choose to support BTS—they are the protagonists of the music industry who constantly fight against the villains of prejudice and oppression. Armed with their songs and stage performances, they seem committed to fighting until the very end.

●

Didn't I tell you that
I said we would win

I've been here, and
You've come to me

The day I despise being myself
The day I wish to be gone forever
Let's build a door in your heart
When you open that door and go in
A place will be waiting for you

It's okay to believe,
It'll comfort you, this Magic Shop

I always wanted to be the best
So, I was always impatient and anxious
Comparing myself to others as a daily routine
Choking on my own greed that used to be a weapon
But now I think back, and the truth is
Maybe I wasn't trying to be the best
Just wanted to console and comfort you
To take sorrow and pain away from you

If I told you I was afraid of everything too
Would you believe me?

You gave me the best of me
So, you'll give you the best of you
You found me and understood
You will find the Galaxy in you

Love Yourself: Tear
Track 7 "Magic Shop"
Released in May 2018

Epilogue

As I was organizing BTS' profiles, I wished I could have kept a lot more of their career highlights. However, I was worried that the book would get too heavy and thick to carry around considering their numerous accomplishments and awards.

In 2018, they showcased their *LOVE YOURSELF*轉*'TEAR'* at the 2018 Billboards music awards as their comeback stage. They were invited to the 2018 Winter Olympics Closing Ceremony, as well as South and North Korea's 2018 Peace concert in Pyeongyang, but due to previously scheduled events they were unable to attend, much to BTS' dismay.

When they were trainees, BTS only slept three hours a day and survived off two packs of chicken breasts a day for a year. There was also a time when they only ate one meal over the course of ten days. They endured such hardships so that they could eventually perform on the world stage, and these anecdotes made me admire their efforts. They showed their fierce willingness to go as far as they can over the walls of the world's prejudices and oppression. BTS are upright and beautiful. As a part of hip hop's resistance, they represent the modernity of the improvised poet's talent, and a genuine love of boys and girls. While the fantasies and whispers are like the rapeseed flowers of Mt. Halla and wildflowers of Mt. Baekdu, BTS is the yellow dandelion that breaks a twinkling head through the pavement and rises to meet the sun.

Watching BTS perform on stage makes me feel like they know how to be free and beautiful; like seven dolphins playfully swimming in the ocean. I am proud that they have become a group that represents Korea, and even at this very moment, BTS is probably shedding their blood, sweat, and tears to reach for an even brighter star in the sky.

Introduced by famous American pop star Kelly Clarkson as the "World's No.1 Boy band", BTS instantly drew the crowd's attention at the 2018 Billboard Music Awards. Considering the infamous American music industry, BTS' success was the key topic of discussion during their comeback interview held at the Lotte Hotel in Sogong-dong, Seoul on May 24th, 2018. At the interview, BTS members talked about their musical preferences, album creation process, teamwork, and their communication with the fans.

First, BTS explained that, "There are a lot of people who listen to our music, but everyone has their own taste. This has always been our concern; the major dilemma being how to make music that suits all the listeners' tastes while maintaining our own identity. Despite this, we have always been doing the music and performances that we wanted to do. We did our best to keep it that way and we got lucky. Also, the pain and suffering experienced while creating a high-quality product was excruciating and the burden was indescribable. We could have just done what we do best and shown the fans a similar style, but we wanted to show them something different every time."

BTS went on to say, "The current trend in the industry is to release singles which decreases the entirety of the Albums, but we tried to keep the intro and outro format and focused on if all the songs within that album work together as part of complete package. We think that is the key to our success, and thankfully, the album turned out how we wanted."

BTS' album-making definitely stands out from other artists. Unlike other artists who simply receive their titles and go on stage, BTS tries to understand the songs through a discussion with the producers. The title "Fake Love", which is included in BTS' 3rd album *Love yourself: Tear*, was created by Si-Hyuk Bang (President/Producer), Pdogg (Producer), and RM (Leader). The trio worked on the lyrics, the composition, and the production of the song.

Other members alongside famous foreign producers also participated in making the other songs. BTS explained, "The company hired talented producers, foreign songwriters, and tried to ease the burden of working with the best." While it could not have been easy to work with just a myriad of different people, it seems like the company tried to make it as smooth as possible.

The teamwork among the members is also a critical element of their success. They are always discussing and helping each other when working on a song, and everyone is open to advice. There is also some healthy competition but all in good faith. When members see each other excelling in a specific area, they become motivated and the desire to make better music grows—this helps the entire team to be more productive. BTS' member V described how, "RM wrote him the lyrics and helped him a lot while he was making the intro of the album."

BTS also included a song called "Heaven", which criticizes endless competition to comfort those who are hurt this phenomenon. Lastly, they love their fans and show this by communicating with their fans consistently. They humble themselves and say that one of the keys to success was their content on social media and Youtube—the content is translated into many different languages to expand their reach worldwide. Their love for their fans is unfathomable.

After the Billboard awards, BTS was scheduled to attend an after party with world-class celebrities. However, they gently declined the invitation because they wanted to share that moment with their fans via social media.

"Why women in their 40s are crazy over BTS"

"I am happy to be a fan of BTS"

Women who are in their 40s, with teenage children, are falling head over heels in love with BTS—the boy group who are taking the world by storm with their charms. When seeing articles about BTS on Korean search engines such as Naver and Daum, surprisingly most of the reactions are by women in their 40s, followed by those in their 30s, and then by fans between the ages of teens to their late 20s. This shows that BTS has a wide range of fans from all age groups.

What is so special about BTS that makes women in their 40s to fall for them? One reason could be that they are influenced by their teenage children. Parents become naturally interested in music that their children listen to. Some of them explain that they have become fans of BTS because of their upright characters, musical talents, and love for their fans. These characteristics of BTS makes the parents believe that BTS is different from other idol groups and that they could be a good influence on their children. BTS' music encompasses topics ranging from school, youth, love, breakups, etc. By sending out social messages to their fans, they have gained a lot of sympathy from the "ARMY" fans in their 40s.

ID 'Kim9****' left a comment on one of the articles saying, "BTS constantly shows humility, love for their fans, and their deep anguish about music, which seems to also captivate middle-aged housewives as fans". Another user with the ID 'whad****' said, "45% of the reactions by women in their 40s are probably mothers who have teenage children who become interested in BTS because their children are crazy about BTS and then later become fans themselves". ID 'this****' said, "BTS members are as old as my nieces. I became their fan in my 40s with my 6th grade daughter. I am so proud of them. During my free time, I watch their videos on Youtube. They are so talented and that must be the reason why they have so many fans from all around the world". ID 'seol****' said, "You must listen to 'Young Forever'. I am close to 50, but this song made me look back at my life and made me cry. It reminded me of my youth. Thank you BTS! I will always root for you guys"

Young Joon Choo (Senior Reporter at Segye Times)

About BTS

Members

Jin (Seok-Jin Kim)
Vocalist
Position: Sub Vocal
Jin was born on December 4th,1992 in Gyeonggi province, City of Gwacheon, Korea.
His blood type is O.

SUGA (Yoon-Gi Min)
Rapper
Position: Lead Rapper
Suga was born on March 9th, 1993 in Daegu Metropolitan City, Korea.
His blood type is O.

J-Hope (Ho-Seok Jung)
Rapper
Position: Main Dancer/Sub Rapper
J-Hope was born on February 18th, 1994 in City of Gwangju, Korea.
His blood type is A.

RM (Nam-Joon Kim)
Rapper
Position: Main Rapper, Leader of BTS
RM was born on September 12th, 1994 in City of Seoul, Korea.
His blood type is A.

Jimin (Ji-Min Park)
Vocalist
Position: Lead Vocal/Main Dancer
Jimin was born on October 13th, 1995 in Busan Metropolitan City, Korea.
His blood type is A.

V (Tae-Hyung Kim)
Vocalist
Position: Sub Vocal, Visual
V was born on December 30th, 1995 in Daegu Metropolitan City, Korea.
His blood type is AB.

Jungkook (Jung-Kook Jeon)
Vocalist
Position: Main Vocal/Sub Rapper/Lead Dancer
Jung-Kook was born on September 1st, 1997 in Busan Metropolitan City, Korea.
His blood type is A.

BTS Timeline

September 2010
Si-Hyuk Bang, Producer and CEO of Big Hit Entertainment, starts an advertising campaign to find members for a new boy group. He finds a teenager rapper, Namjoon Kim (RM) and wants to start a hip-hop group. Bang remembers seeing RM for the first time—"He was already known as a new talent in the underground hip hop scene in Korea. I thought he was as good as a professional rapper." Big Hit Entertainment holds 'Hit It' auditions nationwide.

2010 - 2013
After three years of training, RM, Suga, Jin, J-Hope, Jimin, V, and Jungkook become the final members of BTS.

May 20th, 2013
Big Hit Entertainment opens its official BTS home page.

June 12th, 2013
Debut single album 2 Cool 4 Skool (first of the 'school trilogy' series) is released.
'BTS Debut Showcase' is held at Il-ji Art Hall in Chungdam, Seoul, Korea.

June 13th, 2013
BTS appears on national TV for the first time on the MNET music program MCountdown.

September 11th, 2013
First EP O! RUL8, 2? is released.

September 3rd – October 22nd, 2013
First reality TV program airs in Korea: 'Newcomer Bangtan Boys – Channel Bangtan' on SBS MTV.

November 14th, 2013
BTS wins the 'Best New Artist' award at the Melon Music Awards.

January 16th, 2014
BTS wins the 'Best New Artist' award in the Album category at the Golden Disc Awards.

January 23rd, 2014
BTS wins the 'New Artist' award at the 25th High 1 Seoul Music Awards.

February 12th, 2014
The second EP Skool Luv Affair is released.
BTS wins the 'New Artist' award in the Group category at the 3rd Gaon chart 2013 K-Pop Awards.

BTS Timeline

March 29th, 2014
BTS' fan base ARMY holds its first official meeting: '2014 BTS: 1st Fan Meeting MUSTER'.

May 14th, 2014
Album Skool Luv Affair Special Edition is re-released.

June 4th, 2014
First Japanese single "No More Dream" debuts at number six on the Oricon Singles Weekly Chart.

July 16th, 2014
The second Japanese single, "Boy in Luv", ranks number 4 on the Oricon Singles Weekly Chart.

July 2014
BTS starts filming Mnet's reality program 'BTS American Hustle Life' in Los Angeles.

August 20th, 2014
BTS' first full-length studio album Dark & Wild is released.

October 17th – 19th, 2014
BTS' first concert is held at Yes 24 Live Hall.
Three-day Concert Tour in Asia takes place. BTS visits Japan, Philippines, Singapore, and Thailand.

November 19th, 2014
The third Japanese single "Danger" ranks number 5 on the Oricon Singles Weekly Chart. This makes all of BTS' singles in the top 10 list.

December 24th, 2014
First Japanese studio album Wake Up ranks number 3 on the Oricon Albums Weekly Chart.

January 15th, 2015
BTS wins their first Best Artist award in the Albums category at the 29th Golden Disc Awards

February 2015
BTS tours in Japan and holds concerts in the following cities: Tokyo, Osaka, Nagoya, and Fukuoka

April 29th, 2015
BTS releases their third EP, The Most Beautiful Moment in Life. Pt. 1. This is the first album in which all seven members have participated in the making of the album by writing the lyrics and/or music.

June 1st, 2015
The fourth Japanese single "For You" hits number 1 on the Oricon Singles Weekly Chart.

November 27th – 29th, 2015
BTS' third concert '2015 BTS Live The Most Beautiful Moment in Life on Stage' is held.
BTS introduces the lead single of their next album RUN during the concert.

November 30th, 2015
BTS releases their fourth EP, The Most Beautiful Moment in Life. Pt. 2. This album debuts at number 171 on the Billboard 200 Albums Chart.

December 8th, 2015
BTS is named 'The Golden Tweet of the Year' for being most tweeted by their fans in Korea.

December 18th, 2015
The fourth EP, The Most Beautiful Moment in Life, Part 2, and its lead single "Run" rank number one on iTunes K-Pop Album chart and K-Pop Song chart.

January 14th, 2016
BTS wins the Best Artist award (Main Award) at the 26th High 1 Seoul Music Awards with The Most Beautiful Moment in Life series.

January 21st, 2016
BTS wins the Best Artist award (Main Award) at the Golden Disc Awards' Albums category.

January 24th, 2016
ARMY holds their 2nd 'Fan Meeting' 2016 BTS 2ndMuster 'Zip Code' 22920.

February 17th, 2016
BTS wins the 'K-Pop World Korean Wave Star' award at the 5th Gaon Chart Music Awards.

March 15th, 2016
The sixth Japanese single "Run" ranks number 2 on the Oricon Singles Weekly chart.

May 2nd, 2016
BTS' second re-release album, The Most Beautiful Moment in Life: Young Forever, is released. Three new singles in the album, "Fire", "Epilogue: Young Forever", and "Save Me" rank number 1, 2, and 3 on the World Digital Songs chart.

May 7th, 2016
Fourth concert '2016 BTS Live The Most Beautiful Moment in Life: Epilogue' is held at the famous Olympic Gymnastics Arena in Seoul, Korea.

BTS Timeline

June 2016
Asia Concert Tour: 13 concerts in 10 cities in 7 countries that include Taiwan, Macao, China, Japan, Philippines, and Thailand.

July 31st, 2016
BTS wins the 'Singer Award' at the 44th Korea Broadcasting Awards.

October 10th, 2016
The second full-length studio album Wings is released. For the first time, each member has his solo song included in the album.

With this album, BTS top all music charts and win first place in all the music programs in Korea.

The album sells 750,000 copies within two months and becomes the best-selling album of 2016 on Gaon Chart.

It also debuts at number 26 on the Billboard 200 Albums chart, which places BTS as the highest ranking Korean artist and the second highest Asian on the list.

Other accomplishments include:

Number 62 on the Official Albums chart in the UK

Number 16 on the Indie's Album chart

Number 1 on Japan's Tower Record Albums Weekly chart

Number 1 on the Chinese music video sharing site Yin Yue Tai's Korea District Weekly chart

Number 1 on the world iTunes chart in 97 countries

Number 1 on the Apple Music chart in the US

October 27th, 2016
BTS receives the Ministry of Culture, Sports, and Tourism's Minister Award at the 2017 Korean Popular Culture and Arts Awards ceremony.

November 12th – 13th, 2016
Over 38,000 fans gather for ARMY's third meeting '2016 BTS 3rd Muster Army. Zip+' held at the Gocheok Sky Dome in Seoul, Korea.

November 19th, 2016
BTS wins the 'Album of the Year' award at the Melon Music Awards.

December 2nd, 2016
BTS wins the 'Artist of the Year' award at the Mnet Asian Music Awards. This event marks BTS' first Grand Prize in four years since their debut.

January 13th, 2017
BTS wins two major awards at the Golden Disc Awards' Albums category: 'Main Award' for three consecutive years and the 'K-Pop Artist' award.

February 13th, 2017
BTS releases their special album You Never Walk Alone, which had a record-breaking presale of over 700,000 copies, the highest pre-ordered record for the first half of 2017 in Korea.

The music video of the new single on the album, "Spring Day", breaks BTS' previous record of "Blood Sweat & Tears" for the fastest K-Pop music video to reach 10 million views—the new record is 26 hours and 38 minutes.

"Spring Day" also sets a record on the US iTunes charts by debuting at number 8 and being the first K-Pop group to be on the top 10 list.

Another single from the album, "Not Today", ranks at number 11.

The rest of the songs from the album lands in the top 30 singles list.

The album You Never Walk Alone ranks number 61 on the Billboard 200 Albums chart; song "Spring Day" hit number 15 on the Bubbling Under Hot 100 Singles chart.

February 18th – 19th, 2017
'2017 BTS Live Trilogy: Episode III. The Wings Tour' is held at the Gocheok Sky Dome in Seoul, Korea.

BTS' World Concert Tour takes place with seven concerts in five cities in four countries that include Chile, Brazil, and the United States.

April 2017
BTS is honored by the 9th Shorty Awards as the Fourteenth 'Most Influential People on Social Media'. Other winners include Beyonce (number 1), Donald Trump (number 6), and Barack Obama (number 12).

May 2017
BTS wins the 'Top Social Artist' award at the 2017 Billboard Music Awards held in Las Vegas, Nevada in the United States and becomes the first K-Pop artist to be invited to the ceremony and to win an award.

BTS Timeline

June 26th, 2017
BTS is honored by Time magazine for being included in the '25 Most Influential People on the Internet 2017' along with J.K. Rowling and Donald Trump.

September 2017
BTS sets the world record for most Twitter retweets for a male music group with 152, 112 retweets, according to the 2018 edition of the Guinness World Record.

September 2nd, 2017
BTS appears as special guest performers for Seo Taiji's 25th Anniversary Concert 'LotteCard Move: Sound Track vol. 2 Seo Taiji 25'.

September 18th, 2017
BTS releases their fifth EP Love Yourself: Her with "DNA" as its lead single.

September 21st, 2017
'Comeback Show – BTS DNA' airs on MNET

September 23rd, 2017
BTS ranks number 14 on the UK's Official Albums Chart and number 90 on the Singles Chart.

Other accomplishments in European music charts include:

Number 13 on the Sverigetopplistan in Sweden

Number 18 on the Ultratop Belgian Charts in Belgium

Number 19 on the IRMA in Island

Number 56 on the Top of the Music chart in Italy

Number 57 on the Offizielle Deutsche Charts in Germany

On the same date, BTS also tops the iTunes Albums Chart in 73 nations worldwide.

September 25th, 2017
"DNA" debuts at number 85 on the Billboard Hot 100 Chart.

September 28th, 2017
"DNA" ranks as the 38th most streamed song with 1,140 streaming on the US Streaming Chart.

October 2nd, 2017
"DNA" reaches number 67 on the Billboard Hot 100 Singles chart.

October 3rd, 2017
"DNA" ranks number 1 on the Japan's Oricon Chart, albums imported from Korea list.

October 12th, 2017
"DNA" music video surpasses 100 million views by 7:23 pm. Since its release on September 18th, 2017 at 6:00pm (KST), it has taken only 24 days and 1 hour for "DNA" to reach 100 million views, becoming the fastest music video by a K-Pop group to reach the 100 million mark.

"DNA" also sets the record of the highest number of views in the first 24 hours among all K-Pop music videos.

Later that same year, new milestones are set with 200 million views reached on December 17th, 2017 around 10:30 am and 300 million views on March 7th, 2018 around 11:19am.

October 16th, 2017
Pre-order begins for BTS' eighth single in Japan, "MIC Drop/DNA/Crystal Snow".
After three days of presales over 300,000 copies are sold.

November 9th, 2017
Love Yourself: Her sets a new record of best-selling album in Korea with more than 1,370,000 copies sold.

November 13th, 2017
BTS' Twitter account @BTS_twt reaches 100 million followers. This is the most followers reported for a Korean artist.

November 20th, 2017
BTS performs "DNA" on stage at the 2017 American Music Awards.

Their performance slot is the second to the end, and BTS is seated at the front row throughout the show. This is a great accomplishment for the group as they are the first Korean artist ever to be invited and to perform on stage. Their first US television debut is introduced by the Chainsmokers' Andrew Taggart who says, "To call these guys international superstars feels like an understatement."

Prior to the performance, BTS stays in Los Angeles for about a week and appears on the major U.S. shows such as The Ellen DeGeneres Show, Jimmy Kimmel Live!, and The Late Late Show with James Corden. They also conduct interviews with Vogue and Rolling Stone magazine.

November 24th, 2017
Remix version of "Mic Drop" is released.

BTS Timeline

The song is remixed by world famous DJ Steve Aoki and featured by rapper Designer.

It debuts at number 28 on the Billboard Hot 100 Songs chart and sets the record of the highest-ranking K-Pop artist.

November 2017
Big Hit Entertainment announces BTS will collaborate with Unicef to start 'Love Myself' anti-violence campaign.

December 1st, 2017
BTS wins three awards including the Best Artist award at the MNET Asian Music Awards.

December 2nd, 2017
BTS wins five awards including the Song of the Year at the Melon Music Awards.

December 8th – 10th, 2017
Over 60,000 fans gather for the three-day concert '2017 BTS Live Trilogy Episode III The Wings Tour the Final' at the Gocheok Sky Dome in Seoul, Korea.

December 11th, 2017
BTS is named the 10th artist on the Billboard's 'Top 10 Artists of 2017' list, behind Ed Sheeran, Bruno Mars, and Drake.

December 12th, 2017
People magazine (issue date: December 12, 2017) introduces BTS as the 'world's hottest boy band' that performed successfully at the 2017 American Music Awards. The featured article describes BTS as the group that has set a record of being 'the first K-Pop artist to be on the Billboard Hot 100 Songs list' and that Hollywood is watching them.

December 13th, 2017
"DNA" ranks number 49 on the 'Billboard's 100 Best Songs of 2017'. BTS is the only K-Pop artist on the list.

December 31st, 2017
BTS performs on Dick Clark's New Year's Rockin' Eve.

January 9th, 2018
Remix version of "Mic Drop" ranks at number 66 on the Billboard Hot 100 Songs Chart.

January 12th, 2018
BTS wins the 'Best Boy Band' award and ARMY is recognized as the 'Best Fan Army' at 'iHeartRadio Music Awards 2018'.

January 13th – 14th, 2018
ARMY holds its 4th official meeting, 'BTS 4th MUSTER [Happy Ever After]' at the Gocheok Sky Dome in Seoul, Korea. 40,000 fans attend the event.

January 15th, 2018
BTS is honored by the Recording Industry Association of Japan as the 'Only Foreign Artist to be certified Double Platinum'. According to the association's official record, "Mic Drop/DNA/ Crystal Snow" has sold over 500,000 copies.

The album is the eighth Japanese single and achieved the highest-ranking K-Pop song on the Oricon's Singles chart.

February 4th, 2018
BTS becomes the first Korean group to be certified gold by the Recording Industry Association of America with the remix version of "Mic Drop" with Steve Aoki and Designer.

February 12th, 2018
The Recording Industry Association of America announces "DNA" has been certified gold on February 9th for selling 500,000 copies, same as the "Mic Drop" remix.

February 28th, 2018
BTS receives the 'Musician of the Year' award at the 15th Korean Popular Culture and Arts Awards. This marks the first K-Pop or Idol group to be honored with the award.

March 8th, 2018
Gaon Chart of Korea announces Love Yourself: Her has set another record with cumulative sales of over 1.6 million copies since its release in September 2017

April 4th, 2018
Big Hit Entertainment receives a 201.4 billion won (about $190 million) investment from Netmarble Games, according to the company's press release. Netmarble is the company that developed and released a mobile game featuring BTS' photos and videos, 'BTS World' in February.

April 6th, 2018
New 'Love Yourself' series, 'Euphoria: Theme of Love Yourself Wonder' is released through social media sites.

Face Yourself ranks number 78 on the Official Albums Chart; number 24 on the Official Albums Download Chart Top 100 list; number 80 on the Official Albums Streaming Chart Top 100 list in the UK.

BTS Timeline

April 10th, 2018
Face Yourself tops the Oricon Daily Albums Chart for six days and the Weekly Albums Chart in Japan.

April 19th, 2018
Third full length studio album, Love Yourself: Tear goes on the pre-order list on Amazon.com (release date is scheduled for May) and ranks number 1 as the best-selling product in the CDs and Vinyl category.

May 18th, 2018
Love Yourself: Tear becomes number 1 on the iTunes Top Albums Chart in 63 countries, including the US and the UK.

"Fake Love" tops the major song charts in 52 countries, including Denmark, Finland, and Chile.

"Fake Love" music video hits the 1,000 views mark within 4 hours and 55 minutes after the release. This breaks the 6-hour record held by Taylor Swift's "Look What You Made Me Do."

May 20th, 2018
BTS performs at the 2018 Billboard Music Awards after winning the Top Social Artist award for the second year running.

May 23rd, 2018
Producer and the CEO of Big Hit Entertainment, Si-Hyuk Bang, is recognized by Billboard as number 73 on the International Power Players list and is included in the Recording Category Power Players list.

May 24th, 2018
'BTS Comeback Show' airs on MNET in Korea.

August 25th – 26th, 2018
BTS World Tour 'Love Yourself' takes off with the first concert held at Jamshil Olympic Main Stadium in Seoul, Korea.

September 5th, 6th, and 8th, 2018 Concert in Los Angeles, California, US

September 12th, 2018 Concert in Oakland, California, US

September 15th – 16th , 2018 Concert in Fort Worth, Texas, US

September 20th, 22nd, 23rd, 2018 Concert in Hamilton, Canada

September 28th – 29th, 2018 Concert in Newark, New Jersey, US
October 2nd – 3rd, 2018 Concert in Chicago, Illinois, US

October 6th, 2018 Concert in New York, US

October 9th – 10th, 2018 Concert in London, UK

October 13th, 2018 Concert in Amsterdam, Netherlands

October 16th – 17th, 2018 Concert in Berlin, Germany

October 19th – 20th, 2018 Concert in Paris, France

V

SUGA

Jin

JungKook

RM

Jimin

J-Hope